J.D.C.A. PRIDEAUX

THE WELSH NARROW GAUGE RAILWAY

A PICTORIAL HISTORY

David & Charles
Newton Abbot · London · North Pomfret (Vt)

ISBN 0 7153 8354 X

© J. D. C. A. Prideaux 1976, 1982

First published 1976
Second Edition 1982

British Library Cataloguing in Publication Data

Prideaux, J. D. C. A.
  The Welsh narrow gauge railway.
  1. Railways, narrow-gauge—Wales—Pictorial works
  I. Title
  385′.5′09429   HE3820

Published in the United States of America
by David & Charles Inc
North Pomfret   Vermont 05053   USA

Contents

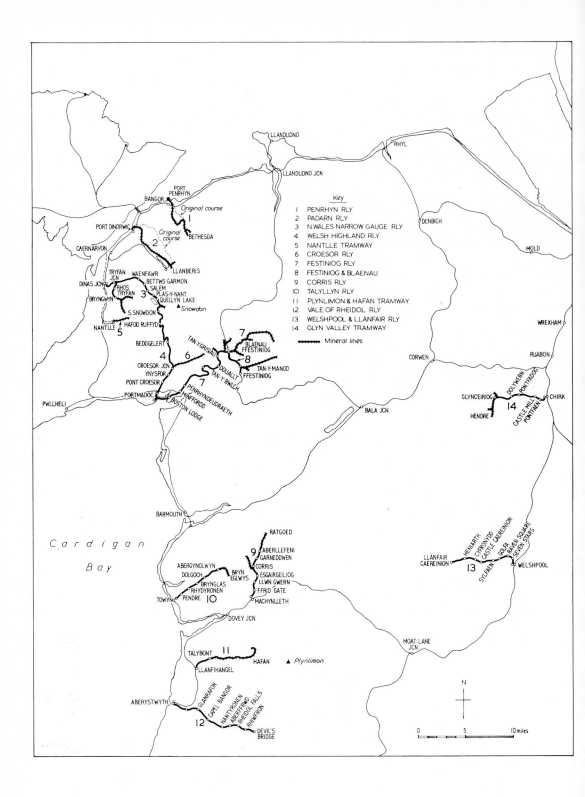

Key

1 PENRHYN RLY
2 PADARN RLY
3 N. WALES NARROW GAUGE RLY
4 WELSH HIGHLAND RLY
5 NANTLLE TRAMWAY
6 CROESOR RLY
7 FESTINIOG RLY
8 FESTINIOG & BLAENAU
9 CORRIS RLY
10 TALYLLYN RLY
11 PLYNLIMON & HAFAN TRAMWAY
12 VALE OF RHEIDOL RLY
13 WELSHPOOL & LLANFAIR RLY
14 GLYN VALLEY TRAMWAY

╪═╪═╪═ Mineral lines

Introduction

Wales suffered much from the industrial revolution. In many places the country is still marred by pit heaps or slate tips. The industrial revolution also produced Wales' own contribution to transport—the narrow gauge railway. In contrast to other forms of development such railways fitted into and did not spoil the country. They brought transport facilities to remote communities, and as a concept were exported throughout the world. Welshmen can take a pride in this achievement.

The Welsh narrow gauge railway was born from a need to carry slate from the quarries to the nearest point where it could be reliably loaded on to ships or barges. In its earliest form the railway was a horse and gravity worked tramway concerned simply with transporting the output of the quarries it served and the occasional back loadings of quarry supplies. Later, when narrow gauge lines had spread to many parts of the Principality the railways adopted steam traction and extended their services to become common carriers of passengers and goods. In the third phase, passenger traffic was abandoned, and the railways deteriorated slowly as freight only lines. The fourth phase, which continues today, has seen the loss of the mineral traffic for which the railways were built and their dependence on summer holiday traffic. All the railways described in this book went through at least part of this four-stage cycle. There have been other narrow gauge lines in Wales—but they were imports rather than the true native product and, fascinating though some of them were—and still are in a few cases—they have had to be omitted here. For example the Snowdon Mountain Railway is purely Swiss in concept and just happens to climb Snowdon rather than an Alp.

Not surprisingly the first railways were built to serve the major slate producing areas—Penrhyn (1801), Dinorwic (1824), Nantlle (1828) and Ffestiniog (1836). These early tramways were later joined by ones serving the smaller production centres, Corris (1859), Croesor Valley (1863) and Glyn Ceiriog (1873). The major distinction between these railways and other horse tramways being built elsewhere in Britain was the gauge, which in the case of the Welsh lines was something near 2ft although it varied slightly and few railways were built to exactly the same gauge. The only railway to differ substantially was the Nantlle built to 3ft 6in gauge, possibly reflecting the influence of George and (brother) Robert Stephenson who held the contract for track laying. The reason why such narrow gauges were adopted is not now known; it was possibly connected with the ease with which small wagons could be taken into the slate works and other confined spaces. The small 2 ton slate wagon able to go anywhere became as much a fixture (and a limitation) of these railways as four-wheeled coal wagons were eventually to become on British standard gauge lines.

The Dinorwic, Penrhyn and Festiniog railways were always in a somewhat different category from the others as the quarries they served produced far more slate. The Dinorwic and Penrhyn were both private tramways owned in each case by the quarries they served. The Festiniog, in contrast, was in a quite different position for it was a public company and as such subject not only to pressure from a number of quarries for better service, but also sensitive to more general public demand to carry passengers and general goods.

The arrival of standard gauge railways in the area during the 1850s and 60s eventually provided the stimulus for development and highlighted the Festiniog's special position. The standard gauge interchange with the Dinorwic and Penrhyn quarries was made at Port Dinorwic and Port Penrhyn respectively, thus protecting the quarry owners' interests in their private railways. The standard gauge proposals further south were for lines direct to the Blaenau Ffestiniog quarries, cutting out the Festiniog Railway completely. Thus it is not surprising that crucial developments took place on the Festiniog. The other pre-requisite was a gifted engineer and here the FR was particularly fortunate in being served by the Spooner family. A preliminary development had been the elimination of inter-mediate inclines which was achieved by tunnelling as early as 1842. Two great achievements were the replacement of horse by steam traction in 1863 and opening to passenger traffic two years later. Most of the eminent engineers of the time thought that it would be impractical to design a 2ft gauge steam engine which was anything more than a toy, and the railway acts then in force prohibited railways of less than standard gauge from being built for passenger traffic. For a time during 1864 the second restriction was successfully circumvented— the railway carried passengers free and charged them heavily for baggage. Strangely, it was neither of these achievements that really caught the public eye, but the spectacular trials in 1869/70 of the railway's new locomotive *Little Wonder*. Then it was not just a case of a narrow gauge railway successfully using steam engines and carrying passengers, it could carry a volume of traffic greater than that handled by many standard gauge railways and not surprisingly was earning broad gauge profits. The whole world came to Portmadoc and went away impressed.

Two railways were built and opened on the new basis of steam haulage and public traffic before the momentous events of 1869/70. The Talyllyn was the first in 1866, promoted by Lancashire cotton magnates seeking an alternative outlet for their money during the American Civil War. Two years later the Festiniog & Blaenau opened—from the start a strategic threat to the Festiniog. It ran as a feeder to the FR until 1883 when the F&B was converted to standard gauge. Both were equipped in the early Festiniog style with small four-coupled locomotives, four-wheeled coaches and wagons no different from those used in horse days.

Only one railway was built in the image of the fully developed Festiniog, the North Wales Narrow Gauge. At the start it reflected the best that the Festiniog could offer with Fairlie locomotives, fine bogie coaches designed by Spooner, and even gravity working of down slate trains. However, only a small part of the whole grandiose scheme was built and that was bankrupt within a year of opening. It was the black sheep of the Welsh narrow gauge family, and this is perhaps why it and its successor, the Welsh Highland Railway, seem so fascinating. The railways built later served less successful, even marginal, quarries and as a result traffic never reached the levels enjoyed by the Festiniog, Penrhyn or Padarn lines. While those railways were each carrying approximately 100,000 tons of slate a year in the late 1870s, the Talyllyn and North Wales Narrow Gauge carried just under 10,000 tons.

This period was the heyday of the railways and it also saw the general upgrading of the remaining horse drawn lines. The first was the Dinorwic tramway (later known as the Padarn), which was rebuilt to 4ft gauge in the early 1840s and introduced steam engines in 1848. This was a false start and the quarry suffered the inefficiency of a two gauge system from then on. The Corris followed a more straightforward policy of easing curves and strengthening track, introducing steam engines in 1878 and using them for passenger services from 1883. In 1878 the Penrhyn brought C. E. Spooner over to lay out a new route avoiding the intermediate inclines. The following year it started operating a special passenger service for its own quarry employees, the nearest either the Penrhyn or Padarn got to operating a public service. The Glyn Valley was rebuilt partly on its original formation and partly over a new route, opening to passenger traffic in 1891. In every case the conversion was followed by a period of adaptation, as stations, equipment and operating practices adjusted to more and different kinds of traffic. A further trend during this period was the conversion of two lines to standard gauge, the Nantlle from 1865 and the Festiniog & Blaenau in 1883.

The heyday of the slate industry, and therefore its railways, was over by 1900. Nevertheless the turn of the century brought a further spurt of activity. The Plynlimon & Hafan was perhaps the most ephemeral of all the railways, for it only lasted three years. Despite this it followed a standard pattern, opening as a mineral tramway, operating a passenger service for a time and then becoming freight only. The Vale of Rheidol and Welshpool & Llanfair opened within six months of each other in the winter of 1902/3. By this stage other traffics were increasingly important, and it was no longer a question of mineral traffic taking precedence with everything else as a sideline. The Welshpool & Llanfair in particular was more akin to a minor branch line. These new railways even had sprung wagons. The final new railway was the Welsh Highland, built in 1922/3, which combined just about all the trends. The shaky North Wales Narrow Gauge was restored and extended over a new route to join the Croesor tramway, part of which was converted from horse operation. As a concept it was at least 40 years too late, but perhaps its promoters should not be entirely blamed. Many false hopes flourished during the 1920s.

With only two exceptions the public carrier role was abandoned during the winter of 1930. The Welsh Highland and Festiniog gave up their passenger traffic at the end of that summer season, to be followed by the Corris and Vale of Rheidol on 1 January, 1931 and the Welshpool & Llanfair some six weeks later. In the last case the closure was delayed as the local communities were particularly good at protesting. From then on there were only two ways forward, either to concentrate on freight traffic or on summer tourist traffic. The goods option was taken by the lines with roadside affinities and the key slate lines. Expenditure was cut to a minimum and the railways slowly ran down. The North Wales Narrow Gauge had already reached this sorry state in 1916 and provided a foretaste of the effect in terms of rotten sleepers,overgrown track and so on. In the end all the railways which took this option closed, the Glyn Valley in 1935, Festiniog in 1946, Corris in 1948, Welshpool & Llanfair in 1956, Padarn in 1961 and Penrhyn in 1962.

Tourist traffic in 1930 was not really sufficient to support a railway. However it was all the Vale of Rheidol now had and the Great Western went out of its way to make it a success. Coaches were completely modernised and the line publicised. This railway was closed throughout the war and after 1945 competed with the Talyllyn for holidaymakers.

The Talyllyn was a remarkable survival. Both the railway and the quarry it served were kept open to avoid increasing unemployment in the area. There were, however, no profits and Sir Henry Haydn Jones (who owned both concerns) could only keep them running on the proverbial shoestring, and the original 1866 equipment had to suffice. There was no insurance and the railway made no returns. Officialdom eventually seemed to forget it. When Sir Haydn died in 1950, L. T. C. Rolt dreamed up the idea of a railway supported by a preservation society and sold this idea both to Sir Haydn's executors and the public. The story since then is well known. The Festiniog, which had fallen into an appallingly derelict state, reopened in 1955 and the Welshpool eight years later. A section of the Padarn was relaid, opening as the Llanberis Lake Railway in 1971, and there are schemes afoot to relay a short length of the Welsh Highland.

Today the railways attract a great deal of traffic and indeed play an important part in the economy of Welsh tourism. All are going through a process of adaptation rather similar to that followed 100 years ago. Locomotives, rolling stock, buildings, operations and attitudes are all having to change. Moreover some lines are expanding. The Talyllyn opened its mineral extension to passengers from 1976. The Festiniog had a portion of its line near Tan-y-Grisiau flooded, and following an epic legal battle has built a completely new route to bypass Llyn Ystradau, the new reservoir and on to a new station jointly operated with BR at Blaenau Ffestiniog. These developments are necessary for the railways to survive, but naturally cost large sums of money. I hope that this book will encourage readers to support the Great Little Trains of Wales and, for those interested, the relevant addresses can be found in the table at the back of the book.

The Snowdonia National Park authorities must sometimes wonder whether they are supposed to conserve the area for the people or from the people. If there isn't someone wanting to carpet it with caravans or dig it up, there's someone else wanting to grow telegraph poles on it or flood it – or less spectacularly but more importantly, someone else again, in his innocent thousands, who just wants to come and look at it. Moorland can take just so many feet, narrow roads just so many wheels; beyond is ruin. A fact long recognised in ecological circles is that if you look for the least damaging means of introducing large numbers of people into wild and fragile scenery, the answer is a narrow-gauge railway.

If God meant us to see Snowdonia, He would have given us flanged wheels and a chimney

The Festiniog Railway bisects the National Park exactly – indeed, it passes through the grounds of the National Park Centre at Plas Tan-y-Bwlch. Primarily a slate-carrying line, it fell derelict in time to avoid becoming British Railways and was rescued by enthusiasts in 1954. Since then the railway has been steadily renovated and restored to the standards of its Victorian zenith, when its engineering ingenuity and professional sparkle set off a miniature world boom in narrow-gauge lines; so that now services operate from Portmadoc over the whole redeemable bottom length of the original track. Above this a section has been lost under the Ffestiniog pumped-storage electricity scheme; and to regain the hill terminal at Blaenau Ffestiniog a deviation line has been put in hand. Half a mile of this has already been built, almost entirely by voluntary, unpaid labour.

Tourism makes a dull crusader for Celtic prosperity: no Welshman will ever die for its flag. But when mineral veins expire, construction projects terminate, marginal agriculture flags, when fringe factories feel the frost and the tap is shut off for subsidised transport, tourism remains, humbly bringing gold without strings. Very shortly, with present trends, Merioneth's only public transport will be steam-operated narrow-gauge trains.

Those who know Snowdonia know that the Festiniog is no mere railway: it appeals on all levels. The Vale of Ffestiniog, through which it runs, was once described by Bertrand Russell as "like an old apocalyptic engraving of Paradise". Paradise may be minimally peopled, but it is surely not without railways. Come and see.

Telephone Portmadoc (0766) 2384

Rheilffordd Ffestiniog · Festiniog Railway

This poster won a prize in the *New Statesman* competition, despite entries from nearly all the major advertising agencies in the country. It aptly summarises the non-enthusiast reasons for supporting the Great Little Trains of Wales.   D. H. Wilson

8

Lush woodland makes an attractive frame to the Talyllyn Railway as a train from Towyn to Abergynolwyn crosses Dolgoch viaduct. The Talyllyn today is one of the Great Little Trains of Wales, all major tourist attractions carrying visitors on a ride into yesteryear behind delightfully antique steam engines, yet all running with an efficiency and enthusiasm that make these lines unique. The Talyllyn was rescued from certain closure by a preservation society in 1951 and set the pattern for the great railway preservation expansion of the last 25 years. But how did it all start? The railways had been there for almost a century, built to carry slate from quarries to the sea, and it is slate that we must thank for the existence of the Great Little Trains of Wales today.

J. F. Rimmer

1 SLATE

Left upper: The bottom of Llechwedd incline, Blaenau Ffestiniog. Balanced inclines were a basic part of the narrow gauge scene, balanced because the descending loaded wagons were attached to a wire rope passing over a drum at the top of the incline and drew the empty wagons up. The dull grey masses of slate waste have become the dominant feature of several quarrying areas. Even the stream had to be put into a culvert as the waste tip encroached.

N. F. Gurley

Left: Wild Aster heads a train of rock and waste along one of the top levels at Dinorwic. Railway working extended right up to the face, whether the rock was quarried (as here) or mined as at Blaenau Ffestiniog. The freshly quarried rock was loaded into small wagons on temporary track, and taken to the dressing sheds. This operation was different in each quarry; it could involve incline working or lifts, and steam, horse or just human haulage. Note the double-flanged wheels on the wagons. These, loose on the axles, coped with any reasonable gauge variation!

R. E. Vincent

Above: The Welsh Slate Company's viaduct, Rhiwbryfdir, Blaenau Ffestiniog. This most interesting photograph was taken sometime between 1879 and 1881 when the LNWR branch was under construction. Rhiwbryfdir house and farm are in the centre and left foreground, with the Rhiwbryfdir Slate Company incline behind. The small building with a siding connection is the Festiniog Railway blacksmith's forge. The Welsh Slate Company's incline is immediately behind the viaduct and the line continues up the valley to serve Llechwedd. Note the line of empty slate and loaded coal wagons waiting to ascend the Rhiwbryfdir incline, and the winding house at the top. Almost the whole valley is now buried under slate tips. Llyfrgell Genedlaethol Cymru

The engine room, Braich Goch Quarry, Corris. Rock was turned into useable slate in rooms such as this. Narrow gauge wagons carried just about everything through these sheds—rock, slab or roofing slate—as well as coal for the boilers if the machinery was steam powered. Many sheds were too confined to take the larger 3 ton wagons, and this, with ease of loading, was the reason why the small 2 ton wagon remained standard. Even a new railway of the 1870s, such as the NWNG, had simple unsprung 2 ton wagons. Llyfrgell Genedlaethol Cymru

The exterior of a dressing shed of similar type to the one shown in the previous photograph. This one is at Penrhyn, with Barclay 0–4–0TW Glyder outside. Rail access to these sheds was either by very sharply curved spurs, or off wagon-turntables. R. E. Vincent

Blanche shunting at Coed-y-Park at the top end of the Penrhyn in 1961. Switches with stub points and moveable diamonds allowed the track to be used by wagons with both single flanged (main line) and double flanged (quarry) wheels. The small Ruston diesel on the right became a common type of quarry engine from about 1935.   J. D. C. A. Prideaux

Jerry M shunting at Gilfach Ddu, Dinorwic, in 1909. The engine's job throughout its life was to shunt wagons for loading on to 4ft gauge transporter wagons—just one aspect of the additional work Dinorwic let itself in for with a two gauge system.
H. L. Hopwood

An early engraving of about 1845 showing a train of empty slate wagons crossing the Cob, with Portmadoc in the background.   Festiniog Railway

2 BY HORSE AND GRAVITY

Horse tramway terminus: New Inn, Glyn Ceiriog before 1886. The booking hut for the tramway can be seen to the left of the tree, otherwise the layout was adapted for freight and changed little over the next 50 years.   Photomatic

Horses were used on tramway feeders long after steam locomotives had been introduced. Some were long lived, and the Ratgoed tramway lasted six years longer than the Corris itself. Here the Ratgoed horse 'shunts' at Aberllefenni slate works.　　　　L&GRP

A gravity slate train passing Dduallt c. 1905. Note the brakesmen sitting on the seventh and eighteenth wagons, and the low proportion of braked wagons (about one in six). Gravity working was the natural adjunct to horse haulage—but was also extensively used by the Festiniog during the steam era. Partly this was a matter of expense. Brakesmen had to be paid but it was cheaper to use the brake power of the locomotive, unless traffic was so heavy that two trains would have been run anyway.　　　*FR Magazine*

Safety also came into it! Gravity trains derailed easily and with impressive consequences. In this upset near Bryn Mawr it looks as if a sheep was the culprit; the unfortunate corpse is being held up by one of the staff.   Festiniog Railway Co.

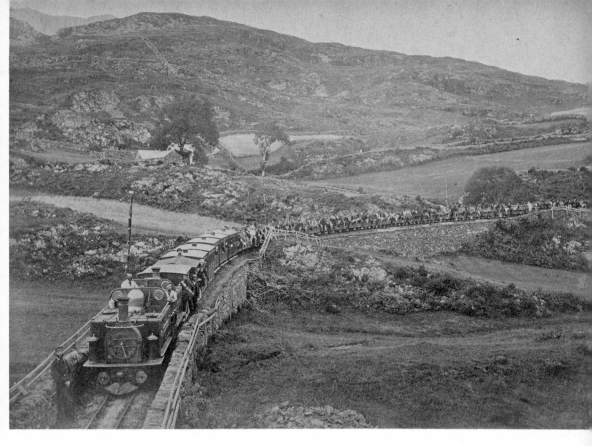

3 HEYDAY

A down train on Creuau curve in 1871. The locomotive is *Little Wonder* and the train consists mainly of the first type of quarrymen's coach, described as 'very precarious' by one contemporary writer.

J. Owen, FR Co.

C. E. Spooner received a medal from the Tsar in recognition of the assistance he, through the Festiniog's example, had given railway building abroad. The growth in narrow gauge mileage throughout the world stemmed from the publicity given to the FR trials of 1869/70.

Prototype passenger train. An early photograph of a
Festiniog train at Duffws, headed by *The Princess* and
made up from the first type of coaches. Note the
refreshment room behind the locomotive, and the
'open class' carriages in use at that time.

Festiniog Railway Co.

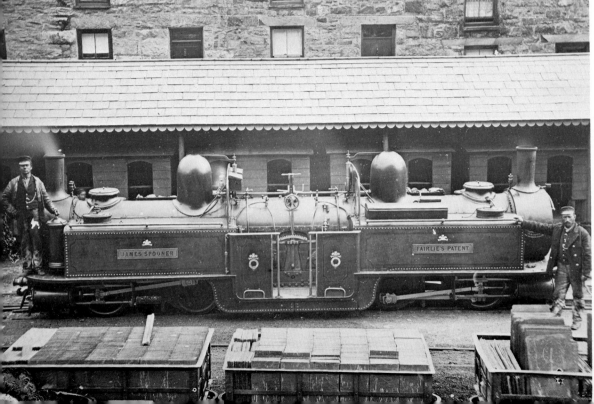

Left upper: Little Giant on a down passenger train at the new Tan-y-Bwlch station in the early 1880s, taken from the same place as the view on page 17. This photograph illustrates the alterations necessary to accommodate new types and volumes of traffic. The station was laid out to allow long trains, of over 100 wagons, to cross. The layout was peculiar, with the goods road in the centre crossing the up passenger line to reach the goods shed and coal sidings. The signalling, level crossing, and stop-block lying on the ground by the centre road are worth noting.

F. Bedford, FR Co.

Left: James Spooner, the Festiniog's second Fairlie, at the east end of Duffws Station c.1880. A rake of wagons which have just worked down the Votty & Bowydd incline stand in the foreground, and quarrymen's coaches are stabled in their daytime shed to the rear. Llyfrgell Genedlaethol Cymru

Above: Merddin Emrys with quarrymen's train at Duffws, between 1879 and 1883. *Little Wonder* stands on the passenger line, right. In *Merddin Emrys* the double Fairlie reached its final form, and it is interesting to discover a photograph which also includes the original engine of the type. By this stage the quarrymen's coaches had been covered on the FR. On the Penrhyn, open coaches survived to run in the very last narrow gauge workmen's train in 1951.

Llyfrgell Genedlaethol Cymru

Top: Blaenau Ffestiniog Exchange (LNWR) station c.1890. The growth period is over and the equipment assumes its most developed form. The locomotive, *Livingston Thompson*, was the last new engine ordered by the company and was generally similar to *Merddin Emrys*. The train is a combined public and quarrymen's down service. The six-compartment bow-sided bogie stock survives to this day as does one example of the final quarrymen's box.

Festiniog Railway

Left: The Talyllyn was the first line to be built as a public railway with locomotive haulage. Both the railway, and the quarry it served, Bryn Eglwys, were speculative ventures which never justified themselves. The equipment provided for the opening proved more than sufficient for the line's entire life as a slate carrier. This is the earliest dated photograph known to the author, taken at Towyn Wharf on 5 March 1900—but the line changed so little that except for the cab on the engine nothing would have been much different 30 years earlier.   H. L. Hopwood

Left lower: Dolgoch running into Towyn Pendre in 1919. This is a picture taken in high summer, with every coach in use.   H. L. Hopwood

Right: The major engineering work on the Talyllyn is the three-arch viaduct over the Dolgoch ravine. Appropriately enough, it is *Dolgoch* which poses on an up train.

Below: Talyllyn on a down train at Quarry Siding early in the century. The train formation is so typical of these lines as to be worth noting—brake van, one composite and one third class coach, and nine slate wagons.

Evening F&B train to Llan at Tan-y-Manod.
Passengers provided most of the traffic, mainly
quarrymen travelling to and from work in Blaenau.
Note the signalling and station buildings, also the
connection to the Craig Ddu quarry right.
Llyfrgell Genedlaethol Cymru

The F&B was converted to standard gauge in 1883,
after which narrow gauge slate wagons from Craig
Ddu were taken to Blaenau on transporters as shown
here. At Blaenau the slate was either trans-shipped or,
if it was for export, handed to the FR for onward
movement to Portmadoc. Transporters were quite
extensively used for a time. The Padarn used them to
carry narrow gauge wagons over the 4ft gauge
section, and the LNWR built a port at Deganwy,
complete with narrow gauge rails, and served it with
trains of transporter wagons from Blaenau.
H. G. W. Household

The Princess at the F&B station at Blaenau. The
small Festiniog engines worked at one time or
another over all the railways which adopted the FR
gauge of 1ft 11$\frac{1}{2}$in, but this is the first photograph
found showing one working on another line as early
as this, c.1880. Llyfrgell Genedlaethol Cymru

Previous page: The Festiniog & Blaenau opened two
years after the Talyllyn, connecting Llan Ffestiniog to
the Festiniog at Blaenau. This superb photograph,
only recently discovered, shows a train on Blaenau
viaduct about 1880. The viaduct gave trouble, and
intermediate trestling was placed to support the spans
even before the line opened. Clearly this was not
enough for the photograph shows no fewer than
three intermediate supports between each pier. The
photograph also clears up long standing doubts about
the track on this railway; it was laid in light flat-
bottomed rail. Llyfrgell Genedlaethol Cymru

North Wales Narrow Gauge country. An NWNG train crosses the Gwyrfai at Plas-y-Nant, with the crags of Craig Cwm Bychan ahead. The train is headed by an 0–6–4T single Fairlie, and coaches 9 and 10 look so new that the year is probably 1893, when they were built by Ashbury C&W Co.   Symans Gems of Wales

Excursion train at Dinas Junction, headed by
Beddgelert and one of the single Fairlies in about
1892. The other Fairlie can be seen at the back of
the train, which includes every coach the railway
possessed until Nos 9 and 10 were delivered in 1893.
Excursion traffic offered a new source of revenue and
was actively encouraged. The Manager was quoted
at the time as saying 'Two specials, consisting of
23 LNWR carriages, containing 800 people, were shot
down at Dinas within an hour, and all these, in
addition to 200 local bookings, I dispatched within
two hours, and brought them all back in the evening'.
Symans Gems of Wales

The Penrhyn Railway was completely rebuilt in 1878 to plans prepared by C. E. Spooner. In its new locomotive-worked form it carried quarrymen, but they travelled in open coaches and not the saloon shown here which was built for Lord Penrhyn himself in 1882. The saloon looks luxurious but with a short wheelbase cannot have ridden well. Nevertheless it was once used for a royal tour of Port Penrhyn.

Royal visit: The Duke and Duchess of York (later King George V and Queen Mary) leaving Dinorwic quarry by the Padarn Railway, 27 April 1899. The special saloon and spruced up workmen's coach contrast with the rows of transporter wagons loaded with narrow gauge slate trucks in the background.

Symans Gems of Wales

Blanche and *Winifred* at Port Penrhyn. *Winifred* was one of the small Hunslet engines used for shunting at Dinorwic and Penrhyn quarries, and at their respective ports, and became a major part of the scene. Note the difference in size between shunting and main line engines.   L&GRP

CORRIS RAILWAY.

Cheap Return Tickets

WILL BE ISSUED FROM

CORRIS

EVERY SATURDAY until OCTOBER 28th, 1893,
to

ABERYSTWYTH,

BORTH, ABERDOVEY,

Towyn, Barmouth,

AND

DOLGELLEY,

AS FOLLOWS
DAY TRIP TICKETS

CORRIS TO	Issued on Saturdays or Mondays. Returning on day of Issue.		Returning on Monday or Tuesday following.	
	1st Class	3rd Class.	1st Class	3rd Class.
Aberystwyth	3s. 6d.	2s. 0d.	5s.	3s.
Barmouth	4s. 6d.	2s. 6d.	6s.	3s. 6d.
Dolgelley	5s. 6d.	3s. 0d.	7s.	4s.
Aberdovey	2s. 6d.	1s. 6d.	4s.	2s. 3d.
Towyn	3s. 0d.	1s. 9d.	4s. 6d.	2s. 9d.
Borth	2s. 6d	1s. 6d.	4s.	2s. 6d.

Available by any of the Ordinary Trains.

J. R. DIX,

Corris, July 1st, 1893.   General Manager.

John Whitridge, "Columban" Printing Works, Oswestry

Corris Railway poster.

The Corris introduced steam passenger services in 1883. In this photograph of Two Bridges, Corris, in the early 1890s, an 0–4–0ST locomotive heads a mixture of four-wheeled and bogie coaches. The Corris locomotives were rebuilt to 0–4–2ST between 1895 and 1900, and the four-wheeled coaches put on bogie underframes by 1900.

Public Record Office, Wehlyn Collection

Old Station, Machynlleth, c.1895. Machynlleth was one of several interchanges where the narrow gauge was near, rather than part of, the standard gauge station. By the time this picture was taken the locomotive was in its rebuilt form and only bogie coaches are to be seen.

Llyfrgell Genedlaethol Cymru

The Corris Railway ran between the road and the river over much of its length; this photograph of Ffridd Wood showing one of its most delightful sections. The railway claimed that this 'exactly resembled the Queen's drive at Balmoral' in its guide for 1895.

Public Records Office—Wehlyn Collection

Llwyngwern Station, the first after Ffridd Wood
where we were invited to 'alight if we wish to visit
the Chamber of Hwmffra Goch'—the cave of a
notorious highwayman. Of possibly more interest to
railway enthusiasts is the complex signalling with
home and distant arms.

Public Records Office—Wehlyn Collection

Train at Corris Station, ready to depart for
Aberllefenni. Two coal wagons stand on the short
siding, with a weighing machine in the foreground,
to cater for local domestic needs!

Llyfrgell Genedlaethol Cymru

Left: GVT *Sir Theodore* with a passenger train on one of the roadside sections.

Below: Sir Theodore with a train of empty granite wagons at Pandy, on the GVT's mineral extension. Originally built to carry slate, it depended on granite which averaged about 50,000 tons a year until the 1930s. Llyfrgell Genedlaethol Cymru

Below: The three Glyn Valley Tramway tram engines, *Dennis*, *Glyn* and *Sir Theodore* at Chirk in the 1890s.
Photomatic

Bottom: Glyn Ceiriog and the GVT from Hafod field, c.1895. The Wynne slate quarries can be seen above the town, but the falls on the river Ceiriog steal the scene. Llyfrgell Genedlaethol Cymru

4 TRANS-SHIPMENT

The quays at Port Dinorwic. At this time (1870s) two
ships were clearing the port every day. Portmadoc
and Port Penrhyn were equally busy. There was a
large export trade, particularly to Germany, but also to
Ireland and as far afield as the USA. Port Dinorwic
and Port Penrhyn trans-shipped slate to the standard
gauge, as well as to ships. and the siding can be seen
in the foreground. Note slate stacked by size, and the
wheelbarrows used to load slate on board.

Llyfrgell Genedlaethol Cymru

A fairly elaborate arrangement at the Maenofferen Wharf at Minffordd (FR). Graded slates stacked left; slates being loaded direct from narrow gauge wagons in the centre. The narrow gauge sunken sidings (for coal etc) are almost invisible in front of the standard gauge coal wagons. Although nearly all the slate wagons are of the slat-sided type known as crate wagons, there is one box wagon in the left foreground. These wagons were really an anachronism on the FR, but were essential on the other railways where they were used for back loading coal to the quarries. L&GRP

The Festiniog had three interchanges—all quite substantial. This is the L&NWR yard at Blaenau in July 1920, with *Welsh Pony* as top shunter.

H. L. Hopwood

Trans-shipping slab by hand at Machynlleth, July 1948. Different quarries specialised in different products and those in the Corris area produced large quantities of slab. This was carried on special donkey wagons and a crane was used for trans-shipment.

S. W. Baker

Trans-shipment at Chirk in 1925. A good example of a simple arrangement, with slate transfer on the left and coal being loaded from the standard gauge on the right. The rail heights are so arranged that wagon floors on both gauges are the same for slate, and the doors on the standard gauge wagon could be dropped to allow coal to be shovelled down with minimum effort. H. G. W. Household

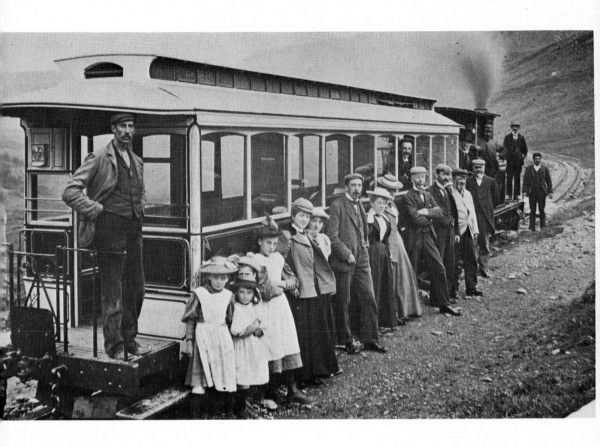

5 THE LATECOMERS

Plynlimon & Hafan passenger train consisting of
Talybont and the only coach. The train is probably
an excursion to the Hafan Incline, quite the latest
thing to do in the remote Leri valley in 1898. This was
the only year in which passenger trains ran on the
tramway, comprising a Monday (market day) service
and excursions. The tramway lasted for only three
years altogether.   Llyfrgell Genedlaethol Cymru

A railway up the Rheidol valley was first mooted in
1861, and eventually opened in 1902. Its sights were
on holiday traffic from the start, though reasonable
loadings from the local lead mines were correctly
anticipated. Here *Rheidol* (lately *Talybont* of the
Plynlimon & Hafan) prepares to leave the
Aberystwyth terminal in Edwardian days. The
streamers suggest carnival time, and the Cambrian's
standard gauge station can just be seen in the
background.   Llyfrgell Genedlaethol Cymru

The same, or a very similar, train pauses at Aberffrwd,
the watering point up the valley. The railway offers
magnificent views of the Rheidol valley. Apart from
this, it is interesting to note the use of separate brake
vans, and the simple manner in which the three
central compartments of the second coach have
been altered into two first class compartments.
                    Llyfrgell Genedlaethol Cymru

Above: Heavy train near Devils Bridge, double headed by *Rheidol* and a 2–6–2T.

Llyfrgell Genedlaethol Cymru

Top right: Summer passenger traffic grew in a most satisfactory way and the line borrowed *Palmerston* from the Festiniog for five summers. Here she approaches Aberystwyth in August 1913.

K. A. C. R. Nunn

Right: Arrival at Devils Bridge. The goods sidings can be seen on the left. Lead was brought here by horse and cart for loading into narrow gauge wagons. The operating practices shown here would hardly have satisfied HM Inspecting Officers of Railways. The final coach is a converted timber wagon—without continuous brakes! Llyfrgell Genedlaethol Cymru

The Welshpool & Llanfair opened in 1903, six months after the Rheidol. Serving an agricultural community it carried little outward mineral traffic, and was in many respects more like English narrow gauge lines than the coastal railways. These two early photographs show Llanfair before 1910. The currugated-iron age arrived in Wales with the Rheidol and Welshpool lines.

Welshpool & Llanfair Railway: H. L. Hopwood

Countess leaving Welshpool on the 11.50 to Llanfair in 1926. Trains started alongside Smithfield Road in Welshpool and until 1913 the station was not even fenced off from the road. The same locomotive is shown, below, approaching Welshpool with the 09.35 from Llanfair. K. A. C. R. Nunn

6 EQUIPMENT

Basic equipment: a small four-coupled tank engine and wooden slate wagons, in this case *Dolgoch* at Abergynolwyn station on the Talyllyn in 1947. In the absence of other traffic such a locomotive could generally handle about 50 empty wagons on the up-journey, which with two trains a day would be sufficient for an annual slate tonnage of 50,000. This was rarely necessary, but two wagons was few by any standards. The quarry had closed the previous year and this was one of the last journeys to clear stock. One wagon appears to have a broken solebar.

S. W. Baker

Little Wonder, the Festiniog's first double Fairlie, and one of the most important narrow gauge locomotives ever built. Its haulage capability was demonstrated during trials in 1869/70 and convinced informed opinion that narrow gauge railways could handle heavy traffic. The double Fairlie became the standard main line locomotive on the Festiniog but was not used on any of the other Welsh narrow gauge lines. This photograph was taken at Duffws around 1880, only shortly before the engine was withdrawn in 1883. Note how the footplating is attached to the bogies rather than the main frame. It swung under the smokeboxes on curves making *Little Wonder* a dangerous engine to travel on.

Llyfrgell Genedlaethol Cymru

Gowrie waiting to depart from South Snowdon NWNG in 1909. The single Fairlie gave the double engine's flexibility with one boiler and one set of cylinders and driving wheels. In the mid 1870s two were built for the North Wales Narrow Gauge and one for the Festiniog. The NWNG liked the type so much that it went back for this one in 1908—the last completely new design for any of the Welsh railways. Reputedly unsuccessful she was sold during the first world war, when the NWNG abandoned passenger services. *H. L. Hopwood*

A more conventional type of 20th century locomotive was this 2–6–2T *Edward VII* built by Davies & Metcalfe for the Vale of Rheidol in 1902. Two further modernised locomotives were built by the Great Western in 1923, and *Edward VII's* sister (brother!) locomotive *Prince of Wales* was rebuilt to the new standards the following year. These three locomotives survive, although *Edward VII* was withdrawn in 1932. *Llyfrgell Genedlaethol Cymru*

Above: Talyllyn third class coach at Abergynolwyn in 1936. The first coaches built for the Festiniog, illustrated elsewhere, had longitudinal seating, and are still used today although they were considered inconvenient a hundred years ago. The Festiniog, Talyllyn, and Festiniog & Blaenau all adopted conventional four-wheeled compartment stock over the next few years, and similar vehicles were built for the North Wales Narrow Gauge in the mid 1870s and for the Glyn Valley 20 years later still. Of these vehicles the Talyllyn's were the largest and in some ways the most advanced. This was just as well for the railway had nothing else until the 1950s!   S. W. Baker

Below: North Wales Narrow Gauge Coach No 1 ready to leave the Ashbury Railway Carriage & Iron Co Works on an LNWR transporter wagon. This represents the most advanced design of the mid 1870s—advanced even by the very best main line standards. It was designed by Spooner and incorporated the experience gained with the first FR bogie coaches in 1871. Subsequent FR coaches built in 1876 and 1879 had many similarities.
                    Festiniog Railway

Right upper: The prize for the least successful coaches on the Welsh narrow gauge must go to the six Hudson bogie vehicles ordered by the Festiniog in 1923 for use on the FR and WHR. This photograph showing one at Boston Lodge in 1925 is the nearest the author has come to a view showing one in use. Some were stripped of their bodies and turned into coal wagons—others rotted until the new regime took over in 1954. The steady decline in quality from the fine vehicles built for FR and NWNG by Spooner reached its lowest point in these things.   H. G. W. Household

Right: The only six-wheeled coaches on the Welsh narrow gauge lines were three Cleminson patent coaches delivered to the NWNG the year after it opened. They form an extraordinary contrast to the sophisticated coach below. The Cleminson flexible wheelbase was initially thought to be a promising way of obtaining a bogie vehicle's flexibility at less cost. Both the Festiniog and the NWNG used it for coal wagons, and the FR vehicle survives to this day.
                    Gloucester RC&W Co

Right lower: Also at Boston Lodge in 1925, this shows the Oakley Family's private trolley—and one of the ubiquitous 2 ton slate wagons. The Oakley trolley was one of a number of semi-private vehicles on the FR in its heyday. By this stage it had become an occasional inspection car.
                    H. G. W. Household

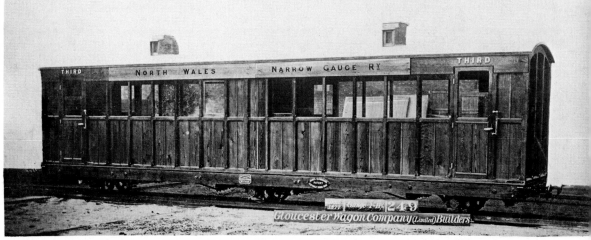

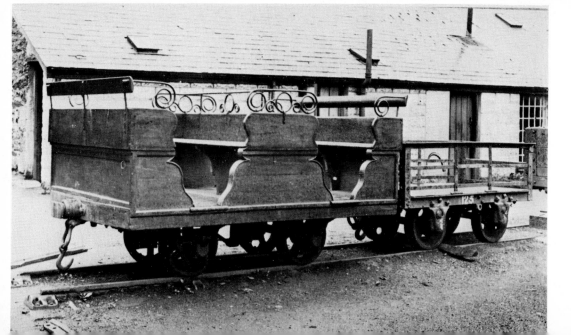

Above: Pendre, Towyn, in 1936. This was the simplest works of all. The buildings, from right to left are: the carriage shed, with a workshop behind, the locomotive shed, the station and a barn used to store hay cut from the lineside and fed to the donkey which pulled the company's delivery vehicle. Today, though most of these buildings remain, the site itself is covered with new sheds to accommodate the great increase in Talyllyn activity.

S. W. Baker

Below: The Glyn Valley Tramway Baldwin 4–6–0T inside Chirk workshop. The GVT, like the Welsh Highland, bought a war surplus Baldwin after the end of the first world war; unlike the WHR the GVT had it extensively overhauled and modified to suit its 2ft 4¼in gauge. If the locomotive is unusual the workshop with its simple equipment is entirely typical.

Lens of Sutton

Right upper: Boston Lodge on the Festiniog was (and is) the most comprehensive and best equipped of the Welsh narrow gauge works. Not only did it build wagons and underframes, two locomotives were built there also. Here is the first, *Merddin Emrys*, following completion in 1879, and absolutely surrounded by her builders, several proudly carrying the tools of their trade.

L&GRP

Right lower: Signalling arrangements of the earlier railways were complex and the FR, Corris and NWNG all had extensive systems. Even the Talyllyn, worked by one engine in steam, signalled its level crossings at the start. This photograph shows FR home/ starting and distant signals at Minffordd.

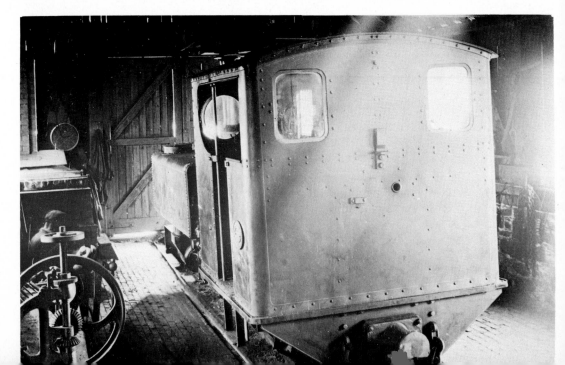

7 NEW HOPE—OLD DELUSIONS

Left: The many proposals to link the NWNG with the Festiniog at Portmadoc achieved reality in 1923 with the opening of the Welsh Highland. Festiniog trains were diverted from their Harbour Station to a new station appropriately called Portmadoc New, where this photograph (taken that first summer) shows a FR train headed by the 0–4–4T *Taliesin* about to leave for Blaenau. On the right hand track stands a Welsh Highland train ready to cross the GWR on its journey to Beddgelert and Dinas Junction. Apparently the two trains left simultaneously and a race regularly developed. Reports from Tom Davies (the FR driver in the picture) insisted that *Taliesin* was the usual victor!

Left lower and below: Russell at Beddgelert during that same first summer on the Welsh Highland. The ex-NWNG locos and coaches were built to a more generous loading gauge than FR stock, and were fitted with air instead of vacuum brakes. The new owners decreed that they should be altered to bring them into line with the FR standards. This was achieved on *Moel Tryfan,* but with *Russell* it was quite a different matter. In the second picture she is shown crossing the GWR in mutilated condition. The irony of the matter was that *Russell* was still too wide to fit the Festiniog, and the butchery was entirely in vain. The Boston Lodge apprentice who cut down the dome was Reg Crick. The night before, he had fired an evening train to Beddgelert, a job which involved lodging there. The lodgings were found by the manager on the advice of the postmaster, but were hardly ideal. Reg and his driver hunted bed bugs for half the night and, after the bugs had won, spent the rest of the night on a garage floor. Was he still itching when he flanged that dome?

L&GRP; S. W. Baker

Princess on the 2.10 to Dinas at Ynysfor, April 1926. Early hopes on the Welsh Highland were soon dashed. The winter service was abandoned as early as 1924, though resumed in skeleton form from time to time later. The reason was all too obvious—not enough traffic. In this photograph there are three train crew, and a locomotive borrowed from the FR, but no evidence of passengers or freight. By 1930, the position was worse still. The quarries had closed or turned to road and it is astonishing that the railway lingered on until 1937.   K. A. C. R. Nunn

On the same day *Moel Tryfan* is seen at Dinas Junction on the daily train, the 12.45 to Portmadoc. Two wagons of coal (probably for Beddgelert), one FR coach and one brake van made up the train. This exemplifies the difficulties the company found in trying to operate a 22 mile route with insufficient traffic for a frequent service. The daily mixed became a jack of all trades, shunting several times en route, and was too slow to attract more than a handful of passengers.   K. A. C. R. Nunn

Many efforts were made to economise. One was to abandon Portmadoc New station and replace it with a Portmadoc (WHR) station north of the GWR crossing. This saved signalmen's wages. It was a pretty gimcrack arrangement with no proper access and only a rough nameboard. *Russell* pauses here during the last year of passenger working—1936.

S. W. Baker

Welsh Highland Railway Train Staff Ticket.

Welsh Highland Railway.

TRAIN STAFF TICKET.

TRAIN No._____(**UP**)

To the ENGINE DRIVER or BRAKESMAN

You are authorised, after seeing the Train Staff coloured **Blue** for the Section, to proceed from

Croesor Jct. to Portmadoc (**New Station**)

and the Train Staff will follow

Signature of person in charge ....

Date ...., 19   (over)

WELSH HIGHLAND & FESTINIOG RAILWAYS.

UP TRAINS.

Report of 12 45' Train Thursday day the 15' day of March 1928

Name of Engine *Russell* Name of Driver *W H Wms* State of Weather *Frosty*

STATIONS.	Time shown on Time Table		Actual Time of		Minutes late.		Delays due to			Number of Wagons.										Approx. No of Passrs.	
										Attached.					Detached.						
	arr.	dep.	arr.	dep.	arr.	dep.	Traffic	Loco.	Engin-eering.	Slate.	Goods or Coal (open)	Goods covered.	Timber.	Slate.	Goods or Coal (open)	Goods covered.	Timber.			In	Out
	H. M.	H. M.	H. M.	H. M.	M.	M.	M.	M.	M.	L. E.	L. E.	L. E.	L. E.	L. E.	L. E.	L. E.	L. E.				
Dinas Jct.	18 45		12 45																		
Tryfan Jct.																					
Rhostryfan																					
Bryngwyn																					
Tryfan Jct.	1258	1 5	1258																		
Waenfawr	1 10	1 7	1 10																		
Bettws Garmon	1 15	1 15	1 15																		
Salem																					
Plasynant																					
Quellyn Lake	1 30	1 30	1 30																		
South Snowdon	1 38	1 41	1 41	1 42	3	1															
Pitt's Head																					
Hafod Ruffydd																					
Beddgelert	2 5		2 7			2															
Nantmor																					
Hafod-y-llyn																					
Hafod-Garregog																					
Croesor Jct.																					
Ynysfor																					
Pont Croesor																					
Portmadoc (New St.)																					
Portmadoc (Old St.)																					
Boston Lodge																					
Minffordd																					
Penrhyndeudraeth																					
Tanybwlch																					
Dduallt																					
Moelwyn Halt																					
Tanygrisiau																					
Glanypwll																					
Bl. Festiniog L.M.S.																					
Bl. Festiniog G.W.																					

Special occurrences on journey:—

Vm Brake in good order
No Right in Train

N.B.—Delays at G.W. crossing and waiting connections to be noted specially.

Numbers and description of carriages on train, viz. :—
1 Compo van No 9

NOTES—Columns L for Loaded Wagons and Columns E for Empty Wagons.

Signed *D Humphries* Guard from *Dinas* to *Beddgelert*.
" " "
W H Wms Driver from *Dinas* " *Beddgelert*
" " "
" " "

Welsh Highland and Festiniog Railway's driver's report dated 1928.

Above: Even the Festiniog was dragged down. Old operating methods proved too expensive with post first world war traffic, and the old owners were largely bought out by the WHR directors who seemed positively spivy in comparison. Signalling was abandoned, a light railway order sought and quality took second place. With poor morale, and worse coal, services went to pieces. Here, two double Fairlies, streaming smoke, cross at Tan-y-Bwlch in 1925.

H. G. W. Household

FESTINIOG RAILWAY.
NOTICE – This Ticket is issued subject to the conditions and regulations in the Company's Time Tables Books Bills and Notices.

DUFFWS
TO
PENRHYNDEUDRAETH

PARLIAMENTARY 10d.

2444

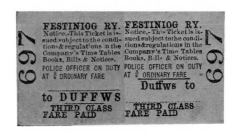

FESTINIOG RY.
Notice.-This Ticket is issued subject to the conditions & regulations in the Company's Time Tables Books, Bills & Notices.
POLICE OFFICER ON DUTY AT ¾ ORDINARY FARE

to DUFFWS
THIRD CLASS FARE PAID

697

FESTINIOG RY.
Notice.-This Ticket is issued subject to the conditions & regulations in the Company's Time Tables Books, Bills & Notices.
POLICE OFFICER ON DUTY AT ¾ ORDINARY FARE

Duffws to
THIRD CLASS FARE PAID

697

FESTINIOG RAILWAY.
NOTICE – This Ticket is issued subject to the conditions on the Time Tables of the Company.

DUFFWS
To
PORTMADOC

SECOND CLASS Fare 2/2

7739

FESTINIOG RAILWAY.
QUARRYMAN'S WEEKLY TICKET 1/1½
Available in Quarrymen's carriages only
NOT TRANSFERABLE
PENRHY
BLAENAU FESTINIOG
Notice.-Issued subject to the conditions and regulations of Company's Time Tables Books Bills and Notices and to the special conditions named on other side

9200

FESTINIOG RLY
DUFFWS

PARCEL 5d STAMP

PAID

No. of Packages.

0828

FESTINIOG RLY
PORTMADOC

PARCEL 4/- STAMP

PAID

No. of Packages

1531

After a time mechanical matters were handed to Colonel Stephens, famous for his association with standard gauge light railways. Management from Kent was not ideal, but he was adept at finding bargains and introduced several progressive ideas. This petrol shunter, photographed outside Boston Lodge loco shed in 1936, fitted both categories. The other railways ignored the possibilities offered by internal combustion locomotives for many years.

S. W. Baker

Other railways sought new power after the first world war to cope with the slate and tourist boom which was confidently expected, and to reduce maintenance on an ageing stud. The Corris ordered this new 0–4–2T from Kerr Stuart in 1921, and she is shown at Machynlleth not long after. Both the first two coaches have been rebuilt with clerestory roofs.

V. Goldberg Collection

The Rheidol passed to the Great Western at the grouping. The large company decided to invest as this photograph at Rhiwfron shows, with reballasted track, new locomotive and fresh paint. Goods and mineral traffic was still significant at this time, but collapsed completely during the mid 1920s.

H. G. W. Household

The GWR also extended the Rheidol to a terminal in the backyard of the standard gauge station at Aberystwyth. One of the two new locomotives heads this 1932 train—complete with steam heating gear which was redundant by then.　　　S. W. Baker

8 FREIGHT TRAIN ONLY

Left: The Great Western was prepared to make bigger changes than the independent companies. On two of its lines, the Corris and the Welshpool, bus competition proved too much for the passenger service and the lines were downgraded to freight only in 1931. From then on it was a matter of seeing what use could be made of them without serious expenditure. These two photographs show the Corris engines that survived, No 3 at Machynlleth and No 4 crossing the Dovey bridge. Lens of Sutton

Above: The Earl at Cyfronydd in 1947. Note the livestock loading ramp in the foreground. The Welshpool passenger service lasted only six weeks longer than that on the Corris, but general goods traffic remained relatively high. It was still unprofitable, and the line was in fact fortunate to survive in any form early GW reports of the 1920s. S. W. Baker

The Earl crossing the Banwy Bridge. Although actually taken on an LCGB special shortly before the line closed in 1956 this picture is typical of workings under British Railways.

N. F. Gurley

Blanche at Port Penrhyn in 1957. While neither the Penrhyn nor the Padarn operated a public service, quarrymen's trains were run until 1951 and 1947 respectively. In one sense therefore the period after this could be classed as 'goods train only'.

N. F. Gurley

Down Festiniog slate train leaving Tan-y-Grisiau in 1940, locomotive *Merddin Emrys*. The Festiniog abandoned its passenger and quarrymen's services on the outbreak of war in 1939, and gravity working followed early the next year.   A. E. Rimmer

The North Wales Narrow Gauge had sunk to freight-only status as early as 1916—although it was subsequently rescued by the formation of the Welsh Highland. Not surprisingly, photographs taken during this freight-only period are very scarce—and this is the best which seems to have survived. *Russell* is seen on a down train at Waenfawr. Already the track is almost hidden in undergrowth and the 'fireman' looks more interested than experienced.   L&GRP

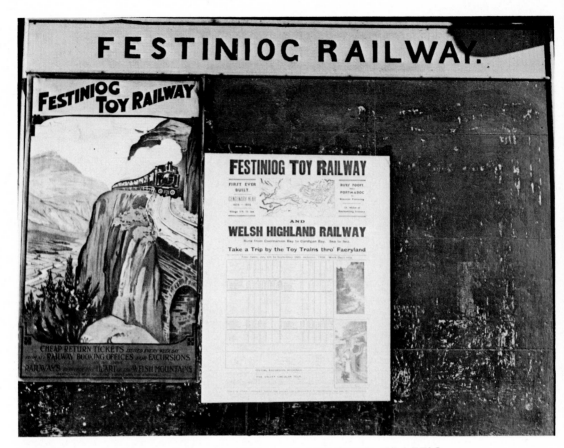

The WHR suspended all services in December 1933. At the last minute the Festiniog leased the line in June 1934, and for the next three years the two systems operated as a single entity, with their sights on summer holiday traffic. The slogan 'take a trip by the toy trains thro' faeryland' grates even today after 20 years of television inanities.   S. W. Baker

9 TOURIST TRAFFIC

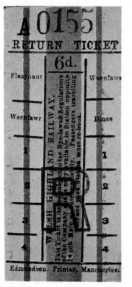

Portmadoc Harbour in July 1936, with *Russell* on the 10.45 to Dinas Junction and *Taliesin* on the 10.20 to Blaenau. In the 1930s both FR and WHR trains ran from Portmadoc Harbour, there being no attempt to revive the New station of 1923.   S. W. Baker

Only the section of WHR through Portmadoc actually ran through town streets. Steam drifts from the whistle as *Russell* approaches the main road crossing in 1936.   S. W. Baker

Above: No. 590 at Beddgelert on arrival from Portmadoc, 1936. Beddgelert became a division point at times, with the trains from Portmadoc and Dinas turning round rather than working through. The two engines used on the Welsh Highland in its last year were *Russell* and the Baldwin 590. This ex War Department engine had been bought at a bargain price in 1923, but never became popular with the men.
S. W. Baker

Right upper: Merddin Emrys arrives at Portmadoc in July 1936. All the Welsh lines could offer the tourist inspiring scenery but none could beat the view towards Snowdonia which a traveller still gets on a fine day from a FR train crossing the Cob.
S. W. Baker

Right: Interchanges with the standard gauge became increasingly important as passenger traffic became more tourist and less local in nature. On the WHR at Dinas you could just cross a platform. Something basically similar happened on the Corris, Vale of Rheidol and GVT, though in each of these cases the narrow gauge was carefully hidden away. The Festiniog had three interchanges ranging from a cross platform arrangement with the GWR at Blaenau, to the two-level arrangement shown here. *Taliesin* leaves Minffordd with a down train, in July 1936.
S. W. Baker

WELSH HIGHLAND RAILWAY
AND
FESTINIOG RAILWAY.

No. 192

WEEKLY SEASON TICKET.
THIRD CLASS,
Available between all Stations,

| From | 19 |
| To | 19 |

Issued to ....

The use of this Ticket is restricted to the person to whom it is granted. Any other person using it will be liable to the penalties incurred by a Passenger travelling without having paid his fare. This Ticket is to be exhibited when required, and is issued on condition that the holder is subject to the Company's Bye-laws and Regulations.

R. Evans

S. E. TYRWHITT,
General Manager.

Issued by ....

Left: A Welsh Highland and Festiniog Railways season ticket.

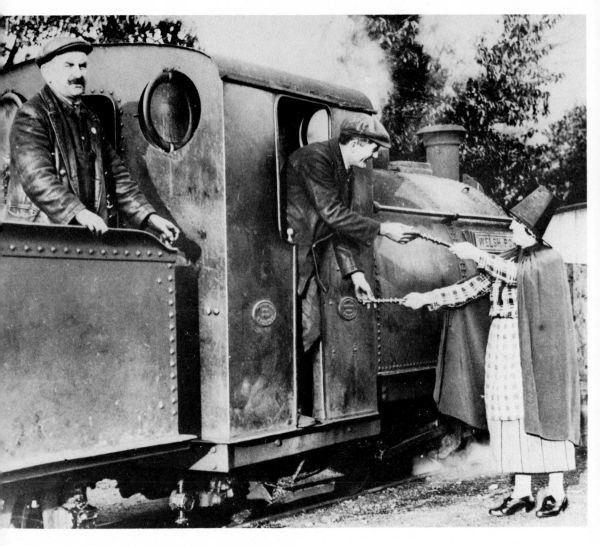

It was an inspired idea to dress Stationmistresses in
national costume. Bessie Jones at Tan-y-Bwlch,
shown here exchanging staffs with the fireman on a
down goods, was the most famous, though the
stationmistress at Beddgelert was similarly attired.
Women were popular as crossing keepers and station
staff—they could be paid less!

L&GRP

The Talyllyn adapted quietly to new levels of holiday travel; it did not seek particular publicity and it did not re-equip in any way. After 1933 it was the only line offering a public passenger service in winter. The layout at Wharf, shown here in 1936 with *Talyllyn* leaving on the 9.25, is still designed purely for slate traffic. There is not even a loop, and the engine could only run round its train by propelling to and from Pendre, or by gravity shunting.

S. W. Baker

Freight traffic abandoned the Vale of Rheidol during the 1920s as the mines closed. The railway closed to winter passengers on 1 January 1931 on the same day as the Corris and from then on has depended entirely on summer holiday traffic. Here GWR 1213, once *Prince of Wales,* waits to leave Devils Bridge on the 4.15 in August 1937. K. A. C. R. Nunn

Dolgoch near Abergynolwyn in September 1947. Services were only operating on three days a week by this stage—and as the railway was entirely dependent on this one locomotive, even this could well be cancelled at short notice. S. W. Baker

Right: If the main line received little maintenance, the sidings had no more than plain neglect. These wagons stand at the bottom of the village incline, Abergynolwyn. S. W. Baker

10 THE END OF AN ERA

Left: Flooding undercutting the Corris Railway embankment by the south pier of the Dovey River Bridge, July 1948. Flooding continued and the line closed in the following month.   S. W. Baker

Left lower: Desolation at Portmadoc Harbour, September 1947. The Festiniog had closed only just over a year before, but Portmadoc had been effectively disused for eight years and conditions were already ruinous. The author well remembers this sight—his introduction to the narrow gauge at three years of age. The station deteriorated for another seven years before the railway was transferred to its present owners.   S. W. Baker

Right upper: The Welsh Highland was requisitioned as wartime scrap, and lifted in 1941/2. The demolition train is shown here in Aberglaslyn pass. A. E. Rimmer

Right: Moel Tryfan was dismantled at Boston Lodge by the summer of 1936, and stayed there until 1954 when she was broken up. The other two Welsh Highland locomotives were left in the shed at Dinas when the railway closed. *Russell* survived to work on industrial lines in Oxfordshire and Dorset, and exists today. The Baldwin 4–6–0 was not so lucky, as this 1942 photograph shows.   A. E. Rimmer

Below: End of everyday industrial steam from the slate age on the North Wales narrow gauge; derelict locomotives rust away at Penrhyn quarries in 1965.
Malcolm Dunnett

Blanche heads a train of empty slate wagons uphill near Minffordd on the Penrhyn Railway in June 1956. Slate workings continued on the Penrhyn until 1962.

R. E. Vincent

The nearest approach to a standard quarry locomotive was a small Hunslet 0–4–0ST, normally cabless, such as *Nesta* shown here on the first level at Penrhyn. There were no fewer than 35 at Penrhyn and Dinorwic, and they also served in other quarries.

R. E. Vincent

The terraced slopes of the galleries at Dinorwic and
Penrhyn have become a feature of the landscape.
Each gallery had its own rail system, normally worked
by one or more 0–4–0Ts. Here the locomotive is
Marchlyn, an Avonside engine bought secondhand
by the Penrhyn in 1936.
Both waste/rock wagons and crate wagons for
roofing slate are visible. This was the typical landscape
of the slate quarry. From the everyday steam railway
viewpoint it was a scene which ended in the 1960s.

R. E. Vincent

A small Hunslet, *George B,* by the weighbridge on the
first level at Dinorwic. A similar engine, *Holy War,* is
shunting sidings in the background. Bullhead rail
was used on tramways worked by locomotives, and
temporary track built up from 3in by $\frac{3}{4}$in (or 1in)
steel bar elsewhere. Early this century there was about
10 miles of bullhead and 35 miles of bar track in the
quarry.   R. E. Vincent

VoR No 8 *Llywelyn* attacks the climb to Aberffrwd during summer 1963. The Rheidol was the first line to concentrate entirely on summer tourist traffic. The GWR rebuilt its existing stock to suit the new role as long ago as 1938. This lead has long been lost, however, and the line has now become an example of how to make the best use of existing assets.   Malcolm Dunnett

11 TODAY

Owain Glyndwr at Aberffryd in the same year. The
tree growth on the right completely disguises the
station's location on a shelf cut in the hillside.
Compare this with the picture on page 45.

Derek Cross

Dolgoch pulls away from Dolgoch Station. Both the original Talyllyn engines have had to be completely rebuilt and are in service. The first coach is the original Talyllyn four-wheeler built by the Lancaster. Wagon Co in 1866, the same year as the engine. Note the absence of door handles since all Talyllyn platforms are on one side, an arrangement also found on the Corris.   J. F. Rimmer

TR *Sir Haydn,* once Corris Railway No 3, on an up
train leaving Brynglas. The train includes old
Talyllyn and Glyn Valley coaches, as well as newly
built stock. Intermediate stations such as this have not
had to change as much as Towyn Wharf, Pendre or
Abergynolwyn.

J. F. Rimmer

Above: Earl of Merioneth leaving Minffordd in June
1968.   J. S. Whiteley/FR Co

Right upper: Linda passes under the deviation to
arrive at Dduallt in the rain. To gain height the new
deviation line here makes a complete spiral in the
fashion of trans-Alpine lines. The deviation involving
over two miles of new railway in difficult country and
including a tunnel, is a massive project for a small
railway. There is plenty of room for more voluntary
help on all the conserved lines.   Festiniog Railway

Overleaf: The Festiniog revival got under way four
years after the Talyllyn. Since then the FR has re-
established its position as the premier narrow gauge
line, carrying by far the heaviest traffic and indeed
becoming one of the top five tourist attractions in
Wales. This photograph contrasts the new and the old.
Mountaineer arrives at Minffordd and crosses *Earl of
Merioneth* on a down train. *Mountaineer* is an engine
built by the American Loco Co for the British Army in
the first world war and remained in France on the
Tramway Pithiviers à Toury until 1965. With larger
wheels and a 2–6–2 rather than 4–6–0 wheel
arrangement, she is a much better engine for main line
use than the Welsh Highland Baldwin to which
Festiniog men had become accustomed between
the wars.
                                         N. F. Gurley

Right: A train on the new line. *Earl of Merioneth* at
Barn site on the deviation in October 1971 after
working a trial train over the new Rhoslyn bridge
(which can be seen alongside the fourth coach). The
wild upland scenery of the deviation will give
tomorrow's traveller the type of view only previously
found on the Welsh Highland between Snowdon and
Beddgelert.
                                         N. F. Gurley

Sir Drefaldwyn alongside the river Banwy. This is a war engine, like the Welsh Highland and Glyn Valley Baldwins, only in this case French-built for German service on the Russian front in 1945.

M. Willis/W&LLR

The Welshpool and Llanfair reopened in 1963. It is a much smaller effort than either the TR or the FR, and runs on an all-amateur basis. The railway has collected a remarkable number of locomotives and coaches, some from as far away as Sierra Leone. In this photograph of *The Earl* at Llanfair, the train is made up of Austrian and ex-Royal Navy coaches. In 1981 the *W&LLR* reopened the section from Sylfaen to the edge of Welshpool near Raven Square.

Lens of Sutton

The Llanberis Lake Railway uses two miles of the Padarn track bed near Llanberis. This 1972 photograph shows *Elidir* (formerly Dinorwic Quarry *Red Damsel*) near Penllyn.

G. F. Gillham

Tabular summary of Welsh narrow gauge railways

Railway	Gauge	Location		Chronology	
Corris Railway	2ft 3in	Machynlleth —Aberllefenni Tramways: Maespoeth —Upper Corris Aberllefenni —Ratgoed	6m 44ch 4m 65ch	Mineral Tramway Common Carrier Freight only	1859–1883 1883†–1930 1931–1948
Glyn Valley Tramway	2ft 4¼in	Chirk —Glyn Ceiriog Mineral extension Glyn Ceiriog —Hendre	8m 63ch c. 3m	Mineral Tramway Common Carrier Freight only	1873, 1886– 1891 1874–1886, 1891–1933 1933–1935
Festiniog Railway	1ft 11½in	Portmadoc —Blaenau Ffestiniog Branches (freight) Quarry feeders (1868)	13m 32ch 70ch 11m 20ch	Mineral Tramway Common Carrier Freight only Tourist †Winter passenger service abandoned 1930	1836–1865 1865–1939† 1939–1946 1955–
Festiniog and Blaenau Railway	1ft 11½in	Llan Ffestiniog —Blaenau Ffestiniog	3m 40ch	Common Carrier	1868–1883
North Wales Narrow Gauge Railways	1ft 11½in	Dinas Jnc —South Snowdon Tryfan Jnc —Bryngwyn Bryngwyn Incline Quarry Feeders	} 9m 35ch } 2m 35ch } approx. 40ch approx. 3m	Common Carrier Freight only Common Carrier Freight only	1877–1916 1916–1922 1877–1913 1914–1922

Traction	Locomotives	Bibliography References	Notes	Society Address
horse 1859–1883 steam 1878–1948	Nos. 1, 2, 3. 0–4–0ST Falcon Engine Co 1878 (rebuilt 1895–1900 as 0–4–2ST) No 4, 0–4–2ST, Kerr Stuart 1921	2*, 4, 7 16, 22	†Official date, unofficially some passengers from 1874. The Corris Railway Society maintain a small museum	Corris Railway Society, Corris, Gwynedd
horse 1873–1888 steam 1888–1935	*Dennis, Sir Theodore.* 0–4–2 Tram Beyer Peacock 1888 *Glyn*, 0–4–2 Tram, Beyer Peacock 1892 ,—, 4–6–0T, Baldwin 1917 (rebuilt & regauged Beyer Peacock 1921)	2, 4 11*		
horse 1836–1863 steam 1863–	*(The) Princess, (The) Prince, Mountaineer Palmerston*, 0–4–0TT, G. England 1863/4 *Welsh Pony, Little Giant*, 0–4–0STT, G. England 1867 *Little Wonder*, 0–4–4–0T, G. England 1869 *James Spooner*, 0–4–4–0T, Avonside 1872 *Taliesin*, 0–4–4T, Vulcan 1876 *Merddin Emrys*, 0–4–4–0T, F.R.Co 1879 *Livingston Thompsom* (later *Taliesin*, later *Earl of Merioneth*) 0–4–4–0T, F.R.Co. 1885 Only Pre-1955 steam locomotive stock is given above. Under new ownership the operational stock has been augmented by *Linda, Blanche* (ex Penrhyn), and *Mountaineer* (2–6–2T Alco Cooke 1917)	1*, 4 14, 15 16, 20 22, 23 24, 25	The railway is open and supported by the Festiniog Railway Society Mileages quoted refer to the late 1860s. The total main line mileage will be different in future following completion of Llyn Ystradau deviation	F.R. Society, 23 Faraday Av, Sidcup, Kent, DA14 4JB
steam	*Scorcher, Nipper* 0–4–2ST Manning Wardle 1868	3*, 4, 14 22, 25	Converted to standard gauge 1883 to form part of Bala–Blaenau Ffestiniog line	—
steam	*Moel Tryfan, Snowdon Ranger* 0–6–4T Vulcan 1875 *Beddgelert* 0–6–4ST, Hunslet 1878 *Russell* 2–6–2T, Hunslet 1906 *Gowrie* 0–6–4T, Hunslet 1908 (name unknown) 0–4–0T on loan 1877	3*, 4, 13 14, 16 17, 22 25	Whole system absorbed by Welsh Highland Light Railway 1922	—

Railway	Gauge	Location		Chronology	
Padarn Railway	1ft 10¾in	Dinorwic Quarry and at Port Dinorwic		Mineral Tramway (c. 1ft 10¾in gauge) 1824–early 1840s	
	4ft 0in	Dinorwic (Llanberis) head of Port Dinorwic incline approx. 7m		Mineral Tramway (4ft gauge) 1840s–1961† †Workman's passenger service was operated 1895–1947	
Penrhyn Railway	1ft 10¾in	Penrhyn Quarry (Coed-y-Park, Bethesda) –Port Penrhyn	approx. 6m 40ch	Mineral Tramway 1801–1962† †Workman's passenger service was operated 1879–1951	
Plynlimon and Hafan Co.	2ft 3in	Llanfihangel –Hafan Mine and Granite Quarry	7m 26ch	Mineral Tramway Common Carrier Freight only	1897 1898 1899
Talyllyn Railway	2ft 3in	Towyn –Abergynolwyn Mineral extension	6m 51ch approx. 60ch	Common Carrier Tourist	1866–1950 1951–
Vale of Rheidol Light Railway	1ft 11½in	Aberystwyth –Devils Bridge	11m 62ch	Common Carrier Tourist	1902–1930 1931–
Welsh Highland Light Railway	1ft 11½in	Dinas Jnc –Portmadoc Tryfan Jnc –Bryngwyn	22m 2m 35ch	Common Carrier Goods only Goods only †Services over former NWNG line restored from 1922 *Winter passenger services finally abandoned 1930.	1923–1936†* 1937 1922–1937
Welshpool and Llanfair Light Railway	2ft 6in	Welshpool –Llanfair Caereinion	9m 4ch	Common Carrier Goods only Tourist	1903–1931 1931–1956 1963–

Traction	Locomotives	Bibliography References	Notes	Society Address
horse 1824–1848 steam 1848–1961	4ft 0in gauge: *Jenny Lind, Fire Queen,* 0–4–0 Horlock 1848 *Dinorwic,* 0–6–0T, Hunslet 1882 *Amalthaea,* 0–6–0T, Hunslet 1886 *Velinheli* 0–6–0T, Hunslet 1895 Many small 0–4–0ST for shunting at port and quarry—1ft 10¾in gauge	4, 14 21*	Two miles relaid to 1ft 11½in gauge and opened as Llanberis Lake Railway from 1971	—
horse 1801–1878 steam 1876–1962	*Edward Sholto, Hilda, Violet* 0–4–0T, De Winton c.1878 *Charles,* 0–4–0ST, Hunslet 1882 *Blanche, Linda,* 0–4–0ST, Hunslet 1893 *Llandegai, Felin Hen, Tregarth* 2–6–2T, Baldwin 1917 (purch 1923) Many small locos, mainly 0–4–0ST, for shunting at port and quarry	4, 14 21*	—	—
steam	*Victoria,* 0–4–0VBT, Slee 1896 *Talybont,* 2–4–0T, Bagnall 1896 *Hafan,* 0–4–0ST, Bagnall 1897	2*, 10	*Talybont* sold to Vale of Rheidol where she was named *Rheidol*	—
steam	*Talyllyn,* 0–4–0ST, Fletcher Jennings 1864 (rebuilt 0–4–2ST. c.1866) *Dolgoch,* 0–4–0WT, Fletcher Jennings 1866 Since preservation the operational stock has been augmented by Corris Railway Nos 3 and 4 (named *Sir Haydn* and *Edward Thomas*) and by *Douglas* (0–4–0WT, Barclay 1918)	2, 4, 6 18*, 19 22	The railway is open and is supported by the Talyllyn Railway Preservation Society	T.R.P.S. Wharf Station, Tywyn, Gwynedd, LL36 9EY
steam	*Edward VII, Prince of Wales,* 2–6–2T, Davies and Metcalfe 1902 *Rheidol,* 2–4–0T, Bagnall 1896 No 7, No 8, GWR Swindon 1923 (named *Owain Glyndwr, Llywelyn* 1956)	2*, 8 12	Operated by British Rail	—
steam	*Moel Tryfan, Russell,* from North Wales Narrow Gauge 590, 4–6–0T, Baldwin 1917 (purch. 1923)	3, 4, 13 14, 17	Railway leased by Festiniog from 1934 The Welsh Highland Light Railway (1964) Ltd has aspirations to reopen a section of the line	WHR (1964) Ltd, Dane House, Runcorn Road, Little Leigh, Northwich, Cheshire
steam	*The Earl, (The) Countess,* 0–6–0T, Beyer Peacock 1902 Since preservation the operational stud has been augmented by *Monarch* (0–4–4–0T, Bagnall 1953), *Sir Drefaldwyn* (0–8–0T, Franco Belge 1944) and a 2–6–2T (Hunslet 1954) from Sierra Leone	2, 5* 9	The Railway is open— supported by the Welshpool and Llanfair Light Railway Preservation Co Ltd	W&LLR, The Station, Llanfair, Welshpool, Powys

Bound for Abergynolwyn. An up train shortly after leaving Towyn.   J. F. Rimmer

Acknowledgements

I would like to thank all the photographers and companies whose work forms the illustrations in the book. I am also grateful to the Festiniog and Talyllyn Railway companies, to the Welshpool & Llanfair Light Railway Preservation Company, and to the Welsh Highland Light Railway (1964) Ltd for providing information. D. M. Francis, Assistant Keeper in the Department of Prints, Drawings and Maps at the National Library of Wales went to special trouble to search the library collection, finding many of the early views from the John Thomas Collection reproduced here. The major debt of gratitude is however to the editors of the *Festiniog Railway Magazine*, and particularly Norman Gurley, not only for allowing magazine material to be used but also for devoting so much of his own time to the project.

Bibliography

1 Boyd, J. I. C. *The Festiniog Railway*. Oakwood Press. Vol 1, 1975, Vol 2 to be published
2 Boyd, J. I. C. *Narrow Gauge Railways in Mid Wales*. Oakwood Press, 1965
3 Boyd, J. I. C. *Narrow Gauge Railways in South Caernarvonshire*. Oakwood Press, 1972
4 Bradley, V. J. and Hindley, P. *Industrial and Independent Locomotives and Railways of North Wales*. Birmingham Locomotive Club (now Industrial Railway Society) 1968
5 Cartwright, R. and Russell, R. T. *The Welshpool and Llanfair Railway*, David & Charles, 1972
6 Cozens, L. *The Talyllyn Railway*. Privately published, 1948
7 Cozens, L. *The Corris Railway*. Privately published, 1949
8 Cozens, L. *The Vale of Rheidol Railway*. Privately published, 1950
9 Cozens, L. *The Welshpool and Llanfair Light Railway*. Privately published, 1951
10 Cozens, L. *The Plynlimon and Hafan Tramway*. Privately published, 1955
11 Davies, D. L. *The Glyn Valley Tramway*. Oakwood Press, 1962
12 Davies, W. J. K. *The Vale of Rheidol Light Railway*, Ian Allan, 1960
13 Deegan, P. *Introducing Russell*. Russell Restoration Fund, 1969
14 Lee, C. E. *Narrow Gauge Rails in North Wales*. Railway Publishing Co., 1945
15 Lewis, M. J. T. *How Ffestiniog got its Railway*. Railway and Canal Historical Society, 1965
16 McKay, J. C. *Light Railways*, 1896
17 Rimmer, A. E. (Editor) *More About the Welsh Highland Railway*. David & Charles, 1966
18 Rolt, L. T. C. *Railway Adventure*. Pan Paperback
19 Rolt, L. T. C. (Editor) *Talyllyn Century*. David & Charles, 1965
20 Spooner, C. E. *Narrow Gauge Railways*, 1871
21 Turner, S. *The Padarn and Penrhyn Railways*. David & Charles, 1975
22 Vignes, M. E. *Etude Technique sur le Chemin de Fer de Festiniog*. Dunod, 1878
23 Whitehouse, P. B. *Festiniog Railway Revival*. Ian Allan, 1963
24 Winton, J. *The Little Wonder*. Michael Joseph, 1975
25 *The Festiniog Railway Magazine*
26 *The Railway Magazine*
27 *The Locomotive Magazine*